D1530473

GOODNIGHT. OBAMA

A PARODY

BY NEW YORK TIMES
#1 BESTSELLING AUTHOR
JEROME CORSI

A POST HILL PRESS BOOK
PostHillPress.Com

ISBN: 978-1-68261-132-6

© 2016 by Post Hill Press
All Rights Reserved

No part of this book may be reproduced,
stored in a retrieval system, or transmitted
by any means without the written permission
of Post Hill Press.

Printed in Canada

Post Hill
PRESS

IN THE GREAT OVAL ROOM
THERE ARE MANY MEMORIES

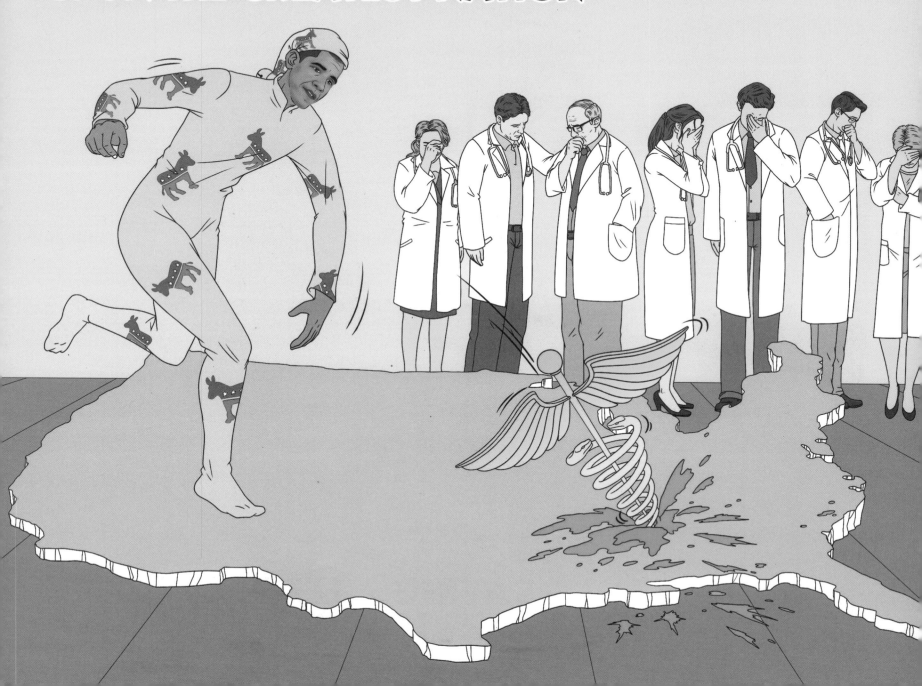

FORCING GOVERNMENT RUN HEALTH CARE UPON THE GREATEST NATION

GITMO DETAINEES
EXCHANGED FOR AWOL CRYBABIES

CROCODILE TEARS OVER GUN RESTRICTIONS

AND THE I.R.S. TARGETING CONSERVATISM

UNITED STATES

Internal Revenue Service Building

GOODNIGHT CONSTITUTION,
BY EXECUTIVE ORDER

GOODNIGHT TALK SHOWS,
CELEBRITY WHORING NOW DONE

AND GOODNIGHT TO ALL THOSE CLINGING
TO THEIR BIBLES AND THEIR GUNS

GOODNIGHT BIRTH CERTIFICATE OF UNKNOWN SOURCE

GOODNIGHT ONLINE VIDEO,
THE SCAPEGOAT TO BLAMÉ

GOODNIGHT PUTIN

GOODNIGHT KIM JONG UN

GOODNIGHT ROSE GARDEN

GOODNIGHT WINGS EAST AND WEST

GOODNIGHT 10 TRILLION IN NEW RECORD-BREAKING NATIONAL DEBT

GOODNIGHT 8 YEARS
OF FUNDAMENTAL CHANGE

GOODNIGHT VOTERS,
TWICE BELIEVING WHAT I SAID